Islam and Sudan

Dan Jahn

raven publications

an imprint of The Raven Group

Islam
& Sudan

The role of "dhimmi" in the failure of Sunni Islam

Towards an understanding of how the implementation of Sunni Islam in Sudan has failed to create a modern nation-state acceptable in human-rights oriented international relations.

Dan Jahn

1st Edition
Raven Publications
an imprint of The Raven Group

Islam and Sudan
The role of "dhimmi" in the failure of Sunni Islam in Sudan

Raven Publications | ravenpublications.com
209 Kalamath Street Unit One Denver Colorado 80223-1343

First eBook Edition: January 2011
First US Print Edition: February 2011

Raven Publications is a trademark of The Raven Group, LLC.

ISBN: 978-0-9833211-2-5

10 9 8 7 6 5 4 3 2 1

To my mom

Dr. Catherine Jahn Bernier

whose encouragement to do anything and everything

has resulted in more than a few surprising projects

and

to James Bernier

whose late nights set an example of what hard work entails

Conclusions......................61

Notes............................67

Acknowledgements

This book wouldn't exist were it not for Dr. John Farina, who started me on a path of a constant search for knowledge and understanding in the religious world despite my lack of any religious leanings, and for the professors at the University of Wales, Aberystywth, whose inquisitiveness into the clash of the worlds of religion and politics provided me a place of study.

Sudan

Preface

On 27 January 2011, more than 99% of Sudanese in the southern part of Sudan voted for independence from Khartoum and the Islamic government. This short book is an attempt to shed light on a particular Islamic belief that proved foundational in the long ideological battle fought in Sudan.

The goal of this book is not to provide an in-depth analysis of the current situation in Sudan, nor is to to provide a lengthy diatribe against Islam. The goal is quite simply to contribute to the discussion facing many in the world today: can Islam "modernize" and form the basis of a nation-state that can exist in harmony with competing ideologies?

Dan Jahn
February 2011
Denver, Colorado

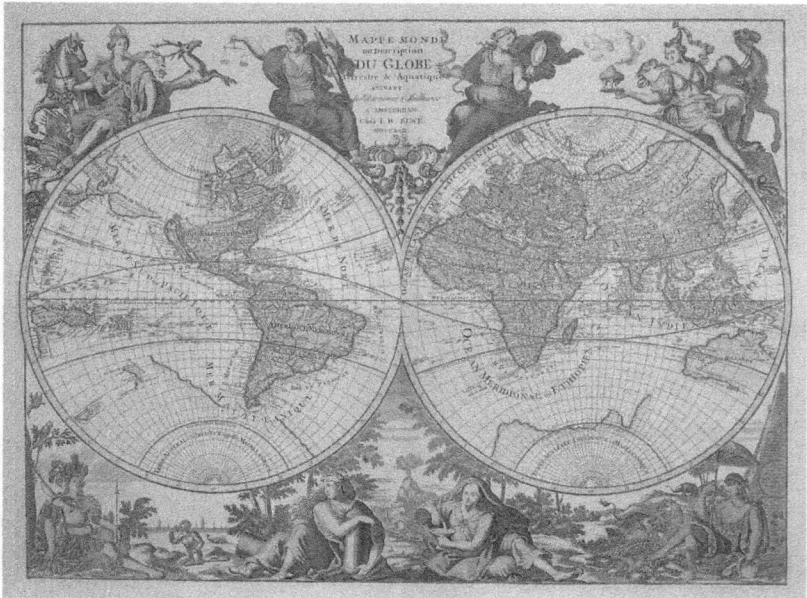

Introduction

There is perhaps no single greater impact on the field of international politics and relations than the varieties of religious experience which play varying roles in dictating the belief structures and social norms which influence interacting people, nations and international organizations.

In some cases it seems that religion will in fact be the one final barrier to attaining peaceful international relations. Why is this? Looking to the *Penguin Dictionary of Politics* as quoted by George Moyser, we learn that "a nation is a body of people who see at least part of their identity in terms of a single communal identity with some considerable historical continuity of union, with major elements of common culture, and with a sense of geographical location at least for a good part of those who make up the nation."[1]

Moyser goes on to point out that religion is part and parcel of what the *Penguin Dictionary* is referring to as 'communal identity.' Thus the very concept of international relations relies on the nations in question arriving at a point of agreement on common principles, in the attempt to create a semblance of that 'communal identity', extrapolated to a 'higher', more global level. This contrived global structure fails miserably however, when one nation has difficulty in meeting the Penguin criteria for a nation, as is the case in Sudan, where Islam appears to be the root cause of conflict in the country.

ISLAM AND MODERNITY

In the modern world, the interaction between Islam and various aspects of politics are crucial to the development of a consistent and useful international relations theory and practice. Many questions can be asked regarding the general theme of Islam and modernity:

- Are Islam and democracy compatible?
- From a Muslim perspective, ca the integrity of Islam be maintained in a democratic society?
- Is an Islamic nation-state a betrayal of Islamic ideals?
- Does modernization necessarily mean 'Westernization'?
- Can Islam come to terms with modern science and technology, if so, how?
- What is the role of Islamic law (*sharia*) in the modern world?
- Can *sharia* can be implemented fairly, successfully, and without fear and anger from the West?

These questions lead me to ask the following single question:

Can Islam serve as the structure for a modern nation-state that based on a form of democracy and conception of human rights which would lead to an acceptance of that nation by the reigning powers of the political world - embodied for the most part in the organization known as the United Nations?

If the current situation in the Sudan is any example, the answer to that question must be a definitive 'no.'

To approach this question more practically, the discussion must be narrowed, and must focus on one issue which is crucial to an understanding of the importance of religion in politics world-wide. Such an examination can be structured along the following lines: a paradigmatic approach to international human rights issues, with a conceptual structuralization based on understanding religious minorities in a religious nation-state. For this discussion, Sudan serves as an appropriate case-study.

HUMAN RIGHTS

The paradigm of human rights is playing an increasing role in international politics and relations, but religious beliefs vary, especially to a point at which religiously derived political systems begin to radically differ on the very concept of human rights. Islam, in particular, affords an entry into this discussion, as an ever increasing religious and political power in much of the world, including that ever-bubbling cauldron the West refers to as The Middle East. To further our discussion, we can look at one particular issue - non-Muslims in an Islamic nation-state - what Muslims refer to as *dhimmi*.[2]

In attempting to more clearly illuminate the role of the Islamic concept of *dhimmi*, a case-study approach serves our purposes best, and the situation in Sudan can be used as a case study of *dhimmi* being applied in a modern context. Specifically, we can examine *dhimmi* as a factor in Sudanese state policy towards the Christians and tribal-religion adherents in southern Sudan, taking a paradigmatic rather than an empirical approach.

The basic structure of this examination is in several parts. In this, the introduction, the topic itself is introduced, crucial concepts and terms are outlined, specific questions are asked and some indication of how these questions can be answered is given. In the second section, attention is given to the concept of *dhimmi* in Islam, by giving some historical background, providing the reader a grounding in the Islamic discourse surrounding religion and politics, and placing the concept of *dhimmi* – both past and present – in context. In the third section, a brief overview of Sudanese history, focusing primarily on the events since 1952, offers the opportunity to discuss the ethno-religious dimension of the people, and the splits and divisions in the society - religious, social, economic, cultural and tribal. The fourth section is the body of this examination, where the above themes can be drawn together and applied to Sudan as a case-study. In the fifth and final section, some conclusions will be drawn regarding the applicability of the concept of *dhimmi* as it relates to human rights in Sudan, thus pointing to some of the bigger issues surrounding Islam and politics in the modern world.

Islam

A brief history, the concept of "dhimmi" and religious minorities

A BRIEF HISTORY OF ISLAM

Attempting to encapsulate the history of Islam would exceed the boundaries of this discussion, but some exploration of the development of Islamic thought surrounding issues of rights, law, sovereignty and the dialectic of religion and politics is necessary in order to more fully understand the position of so called Muslim "fundamentalists". In the exploration regarding issues of nation-states, international relations and human rights in the world today, a brief overview of Islam and the development of the Islamic concept of *dhimmi* can be illuminated, setting the background for the difficulties Muslim "fundamentalists" face in using their conception of Islam as the basis for the political, social, and legal structure of a modern nation-state. Such a state must be accepted by the global community as being in general accordance with United Nations resolutions and international agreements on human rights.

THE NOMADIC BEDOUINS

In sixth century Arabia, the Bedouins were still nomadic, and their tribal lifestyle was fiercely communal, as expressed in the Arabic concept of *muruwah* (courage, manliness, honor, chivalry, loyalty).[3] The *shaykh* (leader) of the tribe held ultimate authority, and all members of the tribe owed fealty to the *shaykh*.[4] The tribes were constantly feuding with one another, and communal identity simply stopped at the tribal boundary. Yet within that boundary, the sense of community was incredibly strong, and later served as a value which Islam drew upon in its attempt to create the umma (ultimate community).[5]

The nomadic lifestyle perpetuated near-poverty conditions for centuries, but towards the end of the sixth century C.E, nomadism had led to trading. The Quraysh tribe based in and around Mecca had become wealthy, and Mecca had become a center for much of the Middle East. Long a center of pilgrimage, Mecca now served as a commerce center as well.[6] In the face of the wealth to be garnered trading, the intra-tribal communal identity began to break down in favor of individual advancement, and the importance of the *shaykh* and the concept of *muruwah* rapidly declined. This period of spiritual stagnation is referred to by modern Muslims as *jahiliyyah*, the "time of ignorance",[7] and indeed in many ways the Quraysh tribe was ignorant of the damage it was doing to itself by discarding its sense of community.

The religious beliefs of the Bedouins were based on worship of world-spirits, expressed through rituals of pilgrimage and sacrifice at shrines scattered throughout the land. There was a belief in a pantheon of gods, albeit with a high god atop the pyramid of spiritual power. The place of pilgrimage to honor the high god was the Kabah, in Mecca, under the guardianship of the Quraysh.[8] This guardianship in many ways contributed to the wealth of the Quraysh, as they used their control of the sacred area to bolster their incomes.[9]

There was no belief in an afterlife, only an ideology based on *muruwah* and *darb*. *Darb* can be loosely translated as "fate" or "time", the ultimate power,[10] and thus the idea of *muruwah*, or courage, in the face of this inescapable fate was a strong one when the tribes were living in relatively poor nomadic conditions and the mortality rate was high. With an increase in wealth however, came a gradual increase in the status of money and material possessions, as materialism replaced spirituality. The ideals of largesse subsumed the ideology of *darb* and *muruwah*.[11]

Simultaneous with the decline in their belief structure was a growing awareness of the belief structures of the surrounding people, with whom the Arabs increasingly interacted as Mecca became a center of trade. The end result was the development of a spiritual inferiority. The Arabs realized that the two other primary cultures in the area - Christians and Jews - both had received revelations and texts from their god. These distinct moral foundations gave both the Jews and Christians a sort of moral superiority over their Arab neighbors.[12] The Arabs no doubt resented this, but as Muhammed would point out, still slid further and further into materialism and moral decay.

THE BIRTH AND EARLY YEARS OF MUHAMMED

Into this maelstrom of spiritual, moral and social crises was born Muhammed ibn Abddullah (c 570-632 C.E.). He was born into one of the clans that had not benefited from the increase in trade, in fact, Muhammed's clan – the Hashimites – saw their fortunes decline.[13] The young Muhammed probably felt the decline in his family's status deeply, and began to realize that under the old system of *muruwah*, his family would have been entitled to a share of the bounty. Under the new capitalism, however, his family and its needs were ignored. This was capitalism without a spiritual basis for morality, and one of the results was complete denial on the part of the culture as a whole of its neglected and often needy families, including the Hashimite clan of Muhammed.

In his twenties, Muhammed married a wealthy business woman, Khadija, and with her wealth came some luxuries, including time for reflection. As tradition and history agree, Muhammed was greatly disturbed by the declining spirituality and lack of community in his contemporaries, and began to retreat to the caves of Mount Hira, to spend time in meditation. As Muslim tradition has it, it was during one of these retreats that Muhammed was visited by the angel Gabriel, who commanded the fear-stricken Muhammed to recite. After further encouragement from the angel, Muhammed began to recite, and the words he received via revelation eventually became written down and collected into the text known as the Quran, an Arabic word meaning "recitation".[14]

Muhammed returned to Mecca, convinced that the god of Abraham - thus the one god of both the Jews and the Christians - was in fact the same as the high god of the Arab tribes, that the multitude of spirits and lesser gods were fictitious, and God – Allah – was displeased at the disrespect shown to him by his Bedouin children. Upon his return to Mecca Muhammed began to preach against what he perceived as the vices of the city: reliance on money and material wealth, pride, arrogance, maltreatment of the poor and general spiritual malaise, calling upon people to become Muslims - to become people who "submit" to God's will. Muhammed proved unpopular with most of the city's inhabitants, and fearful for his followers, sent them to the city of Yathrib, later called Medina, where his beliefs were protected by the townspeople. In September of 622 C.E., Muhammed journeyed to join his followers, and this *hijra*, or "emigration",[15] marks the beginning of the Muslim calendar.

In Medina

During his time in Yathrib, Muhammed made the town the center of the new faith, and thus the name Medina, from the Arabic al-Madina - the City.[16] The difference between the two locations was immediately apparent. In Mecca Muhammed had been simply an outspoken man, railing against the injustices he perceived and the reasons for them, whereas in Medina, Muhammed became a political and military authority as well as a religious leader.[17] It was in Medina that Muhammed laid the groundwork for *sharia* (Islamic Law), which can also be viewed as the mingling of religion and politics, or the establishment of an order based on church and state as one. In Mecca, Muhammed had devoted himself to ideals and ethics; in Medina Muhammed was more concerned with regulating the daily lives of his followers, dispensing advice, presiding over legal matters, and generally running the first Muslim state.

Return to Mecca

Increasing his reach by persuasion, argument and force of arms, Muhammed extended Islam throughout the area, eventually marching back into Mecca in 630 C.E. In his triumphant return to the city, Muhammed instructed his followers to destroy the idols at the Kabah in order to immediately devote the shrine to Allah, the one true god, and simultaneously put down all political and military opposition. Muhammed then returned to Medina, promulgated a written constitution, and died just two years later, in 632 C.E., without appointing a successor. In an incredibly short time, Muhammed had organized a nation out of disparate tribes, established a remarkable monotheistic religious tradition with its own revelatory text, theological underpinnings and ethical doctrines, Perhaps even more important, Muhammed had built a state, with a powerful military, and in that context, Muhammed forged a new cultural identity which gave the Arabs a pre-eminent place in the world, both as a religious people, and as a social, political and cultural power in the Middle East. The religious and political aspects of Islam were, for all intents and purposes, doctrinally inseparable.

SEAL OF THE PROPHETS

Dying without naming a successor can be pointed to as perhaps Muhammed's greatest failure, as it sowed the seeds for the almost immediate split in the *umma*. Muhammed was the "Seal of the Prophets", the last member of the human race to receive direct revelation from God, and Muhammed had implemented that revelation in both religious and political terms. As Bernard Lewis has put it, "... the spiritual function was at an end, the religious function remained; that of maintaining and defending the divine law ... The effective discharge of this religious function also required the exercise of political and military power - in a word, of sovereignty - in a state."[18]

Rise of the Caliphate

Muhammed himself had never claimed to be more than a man, an ordinary mortal who had received revelation, but was not himself divine. Thus, when Muhammed died without appointing a successor, his followers were left with a crisis of leadership. Muhammed's closest friends chose Abu Bakr - one of Muhammed's first converts - to lead them. Abu Bakr was given the title *khalifa*,[19] an Arabic word meaning both successor, deputy, and eventually supreme leader of Muslims, as the term metamorphosed into the institution of the caliphate.[20] Abu Bakr was chosen as much for his age and wisdom as for his early conversion; he decidedly was not chosen for any aristocratic ties, as he was from a rather undistinguished clan, and the same was true of his successor, Umar.[21]

The third caliph however, Uthman ibn Affan, was a member of the house of Umayyad, one of the most prestigious clans of Mecca. Although an elected caliph, he was resented by some Muslims for alleged misappropriation of funds and nepotism.[22] When Uthman decided to produce an authoritative Quranic text, Muslims reacted by assassinating Uthman in his home.

Ali ibn Abi Talib, as a son-in-law and cousin of Muhammed, claimed the caliphate on a hereditary basis, but Ali was believed by many to have had a hand in the assassination of Uthman, and in the midst of massive dissatisfaction, agreed to put his claim to the caliphate to arbitration. This in turn angered Ali's own followers, and these Muslims withdrew from the umma and formed the very strict sect of Islam called the Kharijites, an Arabic word meaning "seceders",[23] and it was one of these Kharijites who later assassinated Ali, ending the period of the "Rightly Guided Caliphs", a period which serves as the normative period for Sunni Islam.[24] Ali's main opponent Muawiya was a member of the Umayyad clan of Uthman, and became caliph after Ali, founding the Umayyad dynasty in 661 C.E., which was to last less than one hundred years, ending in 750 C.E.

THE SHIA AND THE SUNNI

Ali's son Hasan and then Hasan's brother Husain continued to rebel against the caliph, claiming that only descendants of Ali - and thus related to Muhammed - could serve as true caliphs. The party, or *Shia*, of Ali was firmly established, and thus the Shiite Muslim division. When Husain led a revolt against the Umayyads in 680 C.E. at Karbala in Iraq, his defeat was seen as the martyrdom of the Prophet's descendants,[25] and lent a passion and fervor to the Shiite faction that has continued to sustain Shiites through the centuries.

The Umayyad dynasty clung to Islam as for validation, as the caliph's claim to political leadership was rooted in his claim as successor to Muhammed as head of the community, both political and religious. Following Muhammed's model, the caliph exercised complete fiscal, military, judicial and political control of the expanding

Muslim empire, and when the Umayyad dynasty replaced election with hereditary succession, the caliph became an absolute monarch.

The Umayyads moved the Muslim capital to Damascus, and extended the borders of Islam throughout the Middle East, North Africa, Spain and Portugal, and east to the Indian subcontinent. Subsuming foreign cultures, the Umayyad dynasty established Arabic as the lingua franca of the empire, and in replacing local rulers with Arab Muslims, established a Pax Islamica over much of North Africa and the Middle East. The Umayyads adapted the more advanced Byzantium governmental structures to Arabic ideals, and forced this system on all their conquered lands, retaining local communities within an Islamic framework.[26] Within that framework and during this period the four divisions of Islamic society became more pronounced and structured. At the top of the society were Arab Muslims, followed by non-Arabs who had converted to Islam. The third category of citizens were called *dhimmis*, meaning "protected ones", and they were higher in status only over the bottom rung of Islamic society - slaves.[27]

CLASSIFICATION OF HUMANS

Islam also holds mankind to be unique, and worthy of dignity, with that dignity affirmed by Allah: "We have called noble (*karramuna*) the sons of Adam."[28] But Islam does not grant man rights simply by that uniqueness, as does Christian and Jewish theology. All rights of man in

Islam derive only from the promise of Allah to those who totally submit (who become a Muslim) to his will. Thus, those who have not submitted, or converted to Islam, are not fully actualized as humans or even as a part of the divine creation deserving of recognition of rights on a par with Muslims.

How rights are addressed for members of minority communities who find themselves within an Islamic community or vice-versa is an issue of great concern in the modern context, and Islam resolved such situations during the caliphate period by developing its concept of *dhimmi*. Originally, the classification of *dhimmi* did not exist. Instead, the people of the world were broken down into three distinct groups: Arab-Muslims, Ahl al-Kitab or "People of the Book" (essentially Jews and Christians, although this was later expanded to included Zoroastrians, and even Hindus and Buddhists in the Far East), and a huge group consisting of everybody that did not fall into either of the first two categories.[29]

The Umayyad Dynasty eventually grew corrupt, and began to abuse its power. Pious Muslims began to protest that Islam was being undermined by the influx of foreign ideas, and a variety of Islamic movements began to mobilize against the Umayyads. Several Muslim splinter groups joined together, including the Khaijites, along with groups of non-Arab Muslims, resentful of their treatment by Arabs, and non-Syrian Muslims, who felt that they were snubbed by Syrian Muslims. These various movements formed a solid revolutionary body with the support of the

Shiites and overthrew the Umayyads under the leadership of Abu al-Abbas, a descendent of one of Muhammed's uncles.[30]   In 750 C.E. the Umayyad Dynasty collapsed and Abu al-Abbas became the first caliph of the Abbasid Dynasty.

The Abbasids quickly moved to ensure their power by destroying all opponents and even their Shiite allies, establishing the Abbasid Dynasty as a thoroughly Islamic and more particularly Sunni regime. During the Abbasid Dynasty, a combination of increased economic stability, a strong central government and wide-spread encouragement of scholastic and artistic pursuits ushered in the Golden Age of Islam. Under their dynasty the Muslim empire spread even further, and Arabic language and culture displaced local customs and languages wherever Islam entrenched itself. This resulted in a hugely disparate citizenry, and there was suddenly a need for a more uniform code of law, which meant that the law as was currently practiced had to be clarified and codified.

In order to achieve this codification, a community of scholars began to develop, devoted to authenticating and clarifying the *hadith*, the collected sayings and practices of Muhammed, along with statements made in the Quran. It is this group of scholars that led to the creation of Islamic jurists, or *qadis* (judges), and it is these *qadis* who developed the term *dhimmi*.[31]

THE CONCEPT OF "DHIMMI"

The essential basis of *dhimmi* is that although Muslims were required to serve in the military, non-Muslims could pay a tax (*jizya*)[32] exempting them from military service and other duties incumbent on Muslim members of the community. The *jizya* also entitled the *dhimmi* to protection by the Muslim military - thus the designation "protected ones". (In practice, the Umayyad dynasty required even the second category of citizen, the non-Arab Muslims, to pay the *jizya*.) Scholars such as James Piscatori, Majid Khadduri and others have concluded that non-Muslims (*dhimmis*) were second-class citizens under such a system, citing the various restrictions placed upon them by the Islamic government.

Citizens classified as *dhimmi* were basically presumed to agree to the supremacy of Islam, and thus to a position of subordination. In addition to the payment of *jizya*, *dhimmis* were not allowed to bear arms at any time, and were subject to additional social restrictions, including restrictions on their dress, their homes and their movements within the empire. *Dhimmi* men were forbidden to marry Muslim women, the testimony of a *dhimmi* was not admitted in Muslim courts, additionally, *dhimmis* were not deemed as being of the same worth as Muslims when it came to compensation for bodily injury or death of a family member.[33] As regards the political machinery, *dhimmis* were not supposed to be appointed to posts of responsibility, as the "Constitution" of Medina points out in its reminders to rulers.[34] Although these rules were by no means always enforced, they were nevertheless codified by the Abbasids in their codification of the *sharia*, and the concept of *dhimmi* is now part and parcel of the *sharia* looked to by "fundamentalist" Muslims.

The concept of *dhimmi* continued to be upheld throughout the successive Islamic caliphates throughout the Muslim world, and was a key element of the policies of the Ottoman Empire. After the 16th century C.E., when Islam went into retreat, *dhimmi* still played a role in every Muslim dominated environment, including Iran. After World War II, the European colonial empires began to relinquish their holds on colonies that had been formerly under Muslim rule. As these territories become independent, the relatively short period of European domination is rapidly being eclipsed by Islamic resurgence. Islam attempts to reestablish itself at the same time as the world at large is attempting to come to grips with and resolve a code of international human rights, conflicts involving minority groups in predominantly Muslim areas are surfacing as the key to the future of such states as the Republic of Sudan.

The History of Sudan

Background to Ideological Conflict

In order to more clearly understand how the historical Islamic attempt at defining the interaction between religion and politics has impacted Sudan's ability to form a modern nation-state and a society based on "traditional" Islam, a basic knowledge of the geography, history and contemporary social and political structure of the Sudan is required. Sudan is a vast geographical region of northern Africa, extending east to west across the continent, forming a semiarid transition zone between the Sahara on the north and the wet tropical regions on the south. Desert and scrublands predominate in the north, grading into grasslands and savanna to the south.[35]

SUDAN

The Republic of the Sudan takes its name from this geographic region, and is the largest country of the African continent, with a total area of 2,505,813 sq. km (967,500 sq. mi.). The country is bounded on the north by Egypt; on the east by the Red Sea and Ethiopia; on the south by Kenya, Uganda, and Zaire; and on the west by the Central African Republic, Chad, and Libya. The name Sudan is from an

Arabic word meaning "black", and is a reference to the black peoples who historically have inhabited the region, the Dinka, who are the native people of the Republic of the Sudan in Africa.[36]

THE DINKA, THE EGYPTIANS AND THE NUBIANS

Since about the 10th century, the Dinka have inhabited an area on both sides of the White Nile, raising herds of cattle, sheep, and goats, and maintaining a fairly simple social system, headed by chiefs who serve both religious and political functions, serving as priests and peacemakers. The 500,000 Dinka living in the Sudan today speak neither Arabic nor English, preserving a language of the Chari-Nile branch of the Nilo-Saharan family.[37]

From remote antiquity until relatively recent times the northern portion of the territory comprising modern Sudan formed part of the region known as Nubia.[38] The history of Nilotic, or southern, Sudan before the 19th century is obscure, although it is generally believed that Egyptian penetration of Nubia began during the period (circa 2755-2255 BCE) of the Old Kingdom.[39] By 1570 BC, when the 18th Dynasty was founded, the area known as Nubia had been reduced to the status of an Egyptian province, and the region between the Nubian Desert and the Nile River still reverberates with echoes of its murky Egyptian past, as the landscape is dotted with monuments, ruins, and other relics of the period of Egyptian dominance.[40]

The Egyptian rule was ended by a Nubian revolt in the 8th century BCE, and a succession of independent kingdoms was subsequently established in Nubia. Perhaps the most powerful of these Nubian kingdoms was Maqurra, a Christian state which flourished from the mid 6th century CE until its invasion in the early 14th century by Egyptian Mamelukes. There was another powerful Nubian state called Alwa, which had its capital at Soba near present-day Khartoum. Alwa was captured c. 1500 by the Funj, black Muslims of uncertain origin, who established a sultanate at Sannar, and the first Islamic state in Sudan.[41]

THE FUNJ, THE TURKS, THE BRITISH AND THE MAHDI

The Funj eventually emerged as a powerful Muslim state in the Middle East, and during the 16th century the Funj capital of Sannar became one of the great cultural centers of Islam.[42] The period of power was destined to last less than two hundred years, however, and dissension among the leading Funj tribes greatly weakened the kingdom during the final years of the 18th century, ensuring a complete Egyptian victory in 1822, at the conclusion of the war which ensued following Egypt's (at that time a province of the Ottoman Empire) invasion of Sannar in 1820.[43]

As a result of the war, the greater part of Nubia became an Egyptian province, known as the Egyptian Sudan, under Turkish-Egyptian rule. This period of Turkish-Egyptian rule endured for 60 years, and successfully extended the boundaries of the province southward. However, the continuing slave trade and general administrative incompetence of the government contributed to a growing internal unrest. The British appointed General Charles George Gordon as administrator and governor of Egyptian Sudan in 1877, and efforts were made to suppress the slave trade and other political and military abuses.[44]

The area descended into anarchy after Gordon's resignation, culminating in the 1882 revolution led by Muhammed Ahmad (1844-85). In 1880 Muhammed Ahmad had declared himself to be the Mahdi, a mythical Muslim figure who would one day rid the world of evil. The group led by Ahmad rebelled, and began intensive fighting, eventually capturing Khartoum in January 1885, when they killed General Gordon, and gained complete control over the province.[45]

The Mahdi ruled the province until 1885, when the caliph Abdallah at-Taaisha (1846-99) took over, and began an incessant war against the Nilotes in order to expand the territory of Sudan, and also made an abortive attempt to conquer Egypt in 1889. In spite of the caliph's successes at territorial acquisition, the province was collapsing internally, as economic and social chaos reigned.[46] Meanwhile, Egypt had become a virtual possession of Great Britain, and in 1896 the British and Egyptian governments became alarmed at the spread of French influence in Nilotic Sudan, and decided to remove the caliph. The combined military forces of Britain and Egypt, under the leadership of General Horatio Herbert Kitchener (1850-1916), routed the caliph's forces at Khartoum's twin-city of Omdurman on 2 September 1898, and the Anglo-Egyptian victory brought about the complete collapse of the Mahdist movement, resulting in the agreement on 19 January 1899, giving the British and Egyptian governments joint sovereignty in Sudan.[47]

In 1936, the Egyptian government signed a treaty with Britain that confirmed the convention of 1899, over the protests of many Egyptian nationalists, who were demanding the termination of British authority in Sudan.[48] Following World War II, Egyptian nationalists finally influenced the government's attitude towards Britain, and in 1946 the two nations began negotiations to revise the treaty of 1936. These negotiations were doomed to failure due to the lack of compromise on both sides; the Egyptian government demanded complete British withdrawal from Sudan, and the British proposed certain modifications of the existing regime, but in no circumstances would agree to withdrawal.[49]

The situation appeared to have reached a high point of dissension in June of 1948, when the British governor-general in Sudan began consulting with Sudanese officials. The result was that the British governor-general refused to negotiate on the ultimate political status of Sudan, and instead initiated reforms designed to give the Sudanese experience in self-government, and a Sudanese legislative assembly was elected in November 1948.[50] Several political groups continued to advocate union with Egypt and boycotted the election. Dissension constituted a grave error of judgment on the part of these groups, because the assembly was formed, and in December 1950 the legislative assembly was dominated by groups favoring Sudanese independence.

The pro-independent assembly adopted a resolution asking Egypt and Great Britain to grant full self-government to Sudan in 1951. The petition was essentially ignored at the time it was made, and for the next two years the Egyptian government continued to demand British withdrawal from Sudan.[51] In October 1951 the Egyptians denounced both the 1899 agreement and the 1936 treaty, proclaiming Faruk I king of Egypt and Sudan. This state of affairs lasted less than a year however, as King Faruk was forced to abdicate in July 1952, after which Anglo-Egyptian negotiations on the status of Sudan resumed, concluding on 12 February 1953, when the two governments signed an agreement providing self-determination for Sudan within a 3-year transitional period.[52]

In preparation for the upcoming elections, several smaller political parties joined to form the National Unionist Party (NUP), under the leadership of Ismail al-Azhari, and the party began vocally advocating union with Egypt. Made up primarily of modern-educated Sudanese, the party also advocated the formation of an essentially secular state, albeit along the lines of Islam. Because the party had at its heart a platform based on Islamic values, it also received support from the Khatmiyyah, a religious organization which was in turn supported by the Muslim Brotherhood.[53]

At this time the Umma Party was also formed, which advocated a totally independent Sudan. The party was identified with the Ansar organization, which was the politically oriented movement from the 1880s, and was part of the self-proclaimed Mahdi's organization. Sayyid Abd al-Rahman al-Mahdi, the son of Muhammed Ahmad, reorganized the Mahdi movement and incorporated its ideals into the Umma Party of which he became the leader.[54]

"SUDANIZATION"

The 1953 agreement stated that parliamentary elections were to be held, and the first Sudanese parliamentary elections were held late in 1953, in which the pro-Egyptian National Unionist Party (NUP) won a decisive victory, and on 9 January 1954 the first all-Sudanese government assumed office, but the territory was still under the control of Britain and Egypt. The day was designated Appointed Day and marked the official beginning of the transitional period and the "Sudanization" program, designed to replace all foreigners in the government and military with Sudanese.[55]

The "Sudanization" program was completed in August 1955, but the end result was a further disassociation between northern and southern Sudan, as geographic and social differences were highlighted in the program in a bungled attempt to clarify Sudanese uniqueness. Responding to the accentuated differences, a group of southern units of the Sudanese army rebelled on 19 August 1955 but quickly succumbed to government forces.

The Sudanese Parliament quickly took action, and on 30 August 1955 addressed the future of Sudanese integration by passing a measure stipulating that the future status of Sudan would be determined by means of a plebiscite. Acting on this information, both Great Britain and Egypt agreed to withdraw their troops from Sudan, giving a completion date of 12 November 1955, and acted in accordance with this statement. On 19 December 1955 the Sudanese Parliament rejected its own earlier measure and declared Sudan an independent state, totally bypassing the projected plebiscite.

The result was the creation of The Republic of Sudan, which was formally established on 1 January 1956 and recognized by both Egypt and Great Britain. Sudan quickly acted to secure its new-found nation-state status in both the Islamic and secular worlds, becoming a member of the Arab League on 19 January 1956 and joining the United Nations on 12 November 1956.[56]

THE REPUBLIC OF SUDAN

The Republic of Sudan held its first parliamentary elections on 27 February 1958, in which the Umma party won a majority, and the Sudan entered its first independent parliamentary period. The Umma Party formed a short-lived new government on 20 March 1958 which was overthrown just seven months later on 17 November by Lieutenant General Ibrahim Abboud (1900-83), the commander in chief of the Sudanese armed forces. Abboud was thought to be an advocate of an Egyptian unity, but he took no steps towards that goal, instead immediately dismissing parliament, suspending the constitution and declaring martial law. The government was completely restructured with Abboud as prime minister of a cabinet with "Arabization" as its only definable goal. As a direct result of Abboud's abuses and Arab domination, groups of activists in the southern Sudan initiated the civil war which raged in Sudan until 1972, at which point the south was granted some autonomy, in the Addis Ababa agreement. In response to growing rejection of his policies, Abboud resigned in November 1964, and was replaced by a supreme council of state. The council was totally inept, and the resulting chaos led to its easy takeover by Gaafar al-Numayri, ending the second Sudanese parliamentary period in 1969.[57]

Colonel (later Field Marshal) Gaafar Muhammed al-Numayri led a group of radical army officers which seized power in 1969 and set up a government under a revolutionary council with unclear policies. Numayri graduated military college in 1952, and was greatly influenced by the Nasser revolution taking place in Egypt at that time. Numayri was actually implicated in several coup attempts before his 1969 success. Political tension continued; there were several coup attempts during this period. None of the attempted coups had much chance of success, as Numayri ruthlessly crushed his opponents, including the conservative Ansar religious faction and the Communist Party after abortive coup attempts in 1971.

Numayri became the first elected president of Sudan in 1972 and continued to consolidate his power, signing the agreement granting the southern Sudan autonomy and ending the civil war. Numayri initially pursued a policy of radical socialism, by putting forth a new constitution in early 1973, which alienated the United States and its allies. The U.S. attitude towards Sudan at that time was certainly at least partially attributable to the murder of two American diplomats by Arab terrorists in Khartoum in 1973. Numayri turned to the Soviet Union and Libya for support in implementing his new constitution, but several additional coup attempts were made, notably in 1976.

Rumor hinted that the 1976 coup attempts were in fact backed by Libya and by local Communists. Numayri became a bit more pragmatic during the mid-1970s, and looked to Egypt, conservative Arab states, and the West for political and economic aid, and pursued relations with the U.S. and its allies. Numayri took stances in foreign policy that were in line with the U.S., for instance backing Egyptian President Anwar al-Sadat in his peace negotiations with Israel. In fact, Numayri was the only Arab leader to support Sadat, and after Sadat's assassination in 1981, Numayri and Sudan were left out on a limb, anxiously awaiting the wrath of Libya, to which Sudan was considerably more vulnerable now that the Egyptian links were gone. A flood of refugees from Eritrea, Uganda, and Chad were entering Sudan at this time, contributing to the instability of the country, and the rapid depletion of resources by the refugees angered the native Sudanese.[58]

THE SEPTEMBER LAWS - SHARIA

Due to a lack of opponents, President Numayri improbably won reelection to a third term in April 1983, and achieved a sudden jump in popularity by issuing a blanket pardon for some 13,000 prisoners. Numayri then immediately negated this action by announcing the implementation of what has since come to be called the September Laws - a complete and formal implementation of *sharia*, Islamic Law. In direct reaction to this announcement by Numayri, the factions in southern Sudan joined to form the Sudan People's Liberation Movement, with a military arm, the Sudan People's Liberation Army. Ironically, the September Laws provided the needed impetus for the ethno-tribal conflicts in the south to be overcome, giving the various southern Sudanese a focal point around which to rally. The harshness of the September Laws, combined with martial law - imposed in April 1984 in the wake of rising tensions with Libya - continuing food shortages and price increases, and the complete rejection of *sharia* by the non-Muslim south resulted in the overthrow of Numayri in April 1985 by the military. The coup was greeted with some elation, as the military promised a return to civilian parliamentary politics within one year.[59]

Holding true to its self-imposed one year plan, the military pulled back in April 1986, and allowed elections to proceed. Sadiq al-Mahdi (1935-), the great grandson of Muhammad Ahmad, was elected prime minister in the first free election in eighteen years, and Sudan entered its third parliamentary period. The election did not represent an all-Sudanese effort however, as voting had to be postponed in thirty-seven southern constituencies due to a guerrilla war against the Muslim Arab government. The war was instigated by southern Sudanese who rejected the notion of Islamization which they perceived to be the true goal of the Arab north.

The elected government in the north laid plans to draft and approve a new constitution and to hold elections every four years, but continuing severe food shortages, southern rebellion and a mounting debt crisis weakened the government's power to the point of ineffectiveness, and a military coup headed by Brig. Omar Hassan al-Bashir

(1944?) overthrew the Mahdi government in June 1989. Bashir imposed a state of emergency, and a 15-member Revolutionary Council was formed, ostensibly to resolve the emergency. In fact Bashir continues to rule the country with the proverbial iron hand.[60]

IDEOLOGICAL WAR CONTINUES

In its relatively short and brutal history in the modern world, the Republic of Sudan has never had a period of peace and prosperity, rather, the history of Sudan is marked by incessant wars of ideologies, and this state of affairs seems likely to continue under Omar Hassan al-Bashir. Conditions continue to deteriorate as the Bashir regime ruthlessly suppresses political opposition and continues to enforce the strict interpretation of *sharia*, of which one result is the ongoing civil war against the disenfranchised southern Sudanese. Meanwhile, the number of refugees and internally displaced persons continues to swell, and mis-management of government funds and the massive depletion of the country's resources has resulted in hundreds of thousands of Sudanese facing the immediate threat of starvation.[61]

The Role of Dhimmi

A factor in Sudanese state policy

One of the keys to the understanding of *dhimmi* in the Sudan's policies is the implementation of *dhimmi* as part and parcel of an Islamization program based on an interpretation of Islam that scholars and media in the west have labeled "fundamentalist".

REALITY VS. DOCTRINE

There appears to be no official recognition of the concept of *dhimmi* on the part of the Sudanese government, and the word does not appear in any easily obtainable documents produced by the official Sudanese government in Khartoum. When issuing statements on the status of non-Muslims in and around Khartoum or on the official position towards southern Sudanese, there is no mention of the concept or implementation of *dhimmi* laws.[62] However, it is clear from incidents in Sudan during the Bashir regime that the form of Sunni Islam which the government is attempting to institute contains a policy mandating the strict interpretation of *sharia*, and such an interpretation has led and continues to lead to decisions which can be viewed as having a great deal in common with *dhimmi* ideals first codified during the caliphate period.

"Sudanese" Islam

The Sudanese government is explicit in its definition of itself as Islamic,[63] but that alone does not truly clarify the religious and political aims of the current Sudanese government. Several governments in the Middle East define themselves as Islamic, but the actual doctrines promulgated by countries such as Egypt, Saudi Arabia and Syria have not resulted in such a formal implementation of the *sharia*. This is all the more interesting, as the Numayri regime (under which the September Laws were initiated) was quite similar to the regimes in Syria and Egypt which resisted formal implementation of the *sharia*. Sadat, Mubarak and Numayri all came from military backgrounds and were admirers of Nasser's socialist ideas, and all began their stint in government with a clear socialist agenda.[64] While Numaryi shifted to a more explicitly Islamic agenda, Egypt and Syria did not. For instance, in Egypt, Sadat advocated a program of Islamization that was modernist in its method, took a gradual approach to implementing any type of Islamic program, and resisted any attempt to shift his policies towards a more formal or "fundamentalist" approach to *sharia*.[65]

"ISLAMIZATION"

In order to understand how the current program of Islamization is affecting Sudan and where the Sudanese interpretation of Islam and *sharia* sit on a scale of "fundamentalism", we must understand the reasons and the timing of the shift in Numayri's policies. The Muslim Brotherhood was active in Sudan, under the leadership of Hasan al-Turabi, and had been active since the late 1940s, when it emerged as a coalition of a number of Islamic intellectual groups.[66] After World War II, the Muslim Brotherhood in Sudan received some encouragement from the British authorities, who probably viewed the Brotherhood as relatively innocuous when compared with the radical Mahdi movement the British had acted to suppress.

The British chose to suppress the Mahdi Movement by actively courting Muslim orthodoxy, even going so far as to prohibit Christian missionary activity in northern Sudan (although the missionaries were allowed to enter southern Sudan). The result of this policy was the development in the South of an educated, English-speaking elite that resented what was apparently the encouragement in the North of an Islamic identity for Sudan.[67] In the process of developing an Islamic Sudan, the Muslim Brotherhood was tacitly encouraged by the British to develop into a political power because of their intellectual (i.e, "modernized", at least so the British hoped) approach to the process of Islamization. However, the Muslim Brotherhood had to compete for recognition as the party most attuned to the needs of an Islamic population against additional political forces including the Islamic oriented Umma Party.

This competition between religious and politics Muslim groups for recognition continued until the late 1970s. After the coup attempt of 1976, Numayri realized that although he had the power to resist the coup, he did not have the political strength to effectively lead the entire populace. Numayri decided to ally himself with strong Islamic elements in the north, in the belief that this would increase his base of support among the people. Numayri persuaded Hasan al-Turabi, the leader of the Muslim Brotherhood, to participate in a "national reconciliation".[68] Numayri appointed Turabi attorney-general, laying the groundwork for the later announcement of a legal program centered on Islamic values – the infamous September Laws.

Once *sharia* was formally implemented in 1983 with the introduction of the September Laws, Numayri had created the final link in the movement to merge Sudanese nationalism and Islam. By 1983, partly due to the policies of the British, the northern Sudanese had no real identity outside of Islam. The consistent policies of the successive governments based in Khartoum had used the ideal of a united front internal to the culture against an undefined "other", resulting in a definition of the internal culture as Islamic, and predominantly Arab-Islamic. Unfortunately, one result of this definition of what it meant to be Sudanese was the creation of a united southern movement against the Arabized north. Although southern Sudanese have a full spectrum of political ideologies represented in the south, they all have rejection of Arabization and Islam as a key component in their platforms.[69]

"Fundamentalist" Islam

Islam is subject to differing interpretations, as there are widespread variations in the practice and interpretation of any religion or ideology. However, it must be made clear that there are in fact differences in various Muslim "fundamentalist" ideas as well. In Sudan, the fundamentalism which the regime currently practices is on many levels synonymous with the overall concept of fundamentalist Islam. Although scholars can disagree on the exact definition of the term "fundamentalist" and its applicability to any specific movement, the term does serve a useful function in that it embodies a certain set of attitudes which may have a wide spectrum of emphasized ideals. One key idea of fundamentalism is that adherents of a fundamentalist movement hark back to an earlier age, in which the fundamentals of the religion were practiced. Fundamentalists believe that modernity and secularization have undermined those fundamental values, resulting in the need to fight back against the encroaching secular values.[70]

It must also be remembered that the term "fundamentalist" has a specifically Western origin. In Christianity, those who have been labeled fundamentalist are those who look to the text of the Bible for guidance. The Christian fundamentalists state that the word of God as revealed in the sacred scripture defines the whole religion, and any interpretation of that is heresy, and it was on this basis that the term fundamentalism was derived. The term arose in reference to those Christians who fought against theories of evolution, stating that such theories were in direct opposition to the story of creation given in the Bible, and thus the use of a sacred text as an infallible guide has come to be one of the main criteria for defining who is fundamentalist.

The sacred text of Muslims – the *Quran* – has nothing to say about non-believers, i.e., those who do not believe in God – therefore all southern Sudanese who continue to adhere to their traditional tribal religions would be classified outside the authoritative text. The *Quran* only refers to people in Mecca, and divides those people on strictly religious boundaries, and does not refer to "atheists" at all. The *Quran* mentions only monotheists in its delineation of people, and within those boundaries makes a distinction between Jews, Christians and Muslims, and mentions other monotheists such as the Zoroastrians. The ideals of a community expounded upon in the *Quran* thus have little relevance when it comes to constructing ideals for modern nation-states with any degree of plurality in religious orientation.

THE "HADITH"

In Sudan, as in most of Sunni Islam, the idea of what is fundamental to the religion is based on a set of ideals that were developed in the Abbasid Dynasty period. Those ideals in turn were founded upon not just the Quran, but on the Sunna of the prophet Muhammed. The Sunna are the practices of Muhammed, and are collected in the *hadith*, the collection of the sayings of the Prophet and descriptions of his actions collected by eye-witnesses to the Prophet's life. Since Muhammed is accepted as the "Seal of the Prophets", part of the mythology surrounding Muhammed is that although he claimed to be an ordinary mortal and not divine, he was nonetheless perfect in his speech and his actions. The fundamentalism which Sunni Islam claims to be promulgating in its implementation of the *sharia* in Sudan is in fact constructed from a set of ideas developed several hundred years after the death of Muhammed, and extrapolated through a romanticism of the past to the set of ideals the current Sudanese government clings to in defending its strict policies to the western world. Muslims dedicated to this idea of fundamentalism selectively ignore this kind of exegesis, and state simply that they are basing their ideals on Muhammed and the Muslim community of Medina. Of course, as the leader of the Sudanese Republican Party – Mahmoud Taha – pointed out, what was appropriate for seventh century Arabia may not be at all appropriate for twentieth century Sudan.[71]

"Medinan" Islam

The interpretation of Islam chosen by modern fundamentalist and Islamic idealists is not the only one open to Muslims, and Mahmoud Muhammed Taha clarified this point in relation to Sudan. Although most Muslims recognize a difference between the Mecca and Medina period, they hold the ideas originating during the Medina period to be authoritative.[72] It was in Medina that Muhammed set down the framework of an Islamic constitution, and it was in Medina that the first Muslim community was structured. The texts of Mecca and Medina have startling contradictions,[73] but Muslims regard the Medina texts as having abrogated the texts of Mecca. Taha argued that the message proclaimed by Muhammed in Mecca prior to the *hijra* was the more authoritative of the essentially two messages carried in Islam. Arguing that Muhammed at first preached democracy, tolerance, freedom and equality, but refined his message to be more in tune with seventh century Arabic mores when he was summarily rejected.[74] Taha was attempting to draw a clear distinction between true Islam – which we can call 'Meccan Islam' – and Islam as it had been changed to suit the seventh century Arabian Peninsula and subsequently interpreted through the ages – what we will call 'Medinan Islam' – resulting in the strict *sharia*. Taha was judged under the September Laws to be an apostate, resulting in his public hanging on 18 January 1985. His ideas are considered heresy in Sudan, and indeed would probably be considered heresy by many Muslims, but as we shall see they nonetheless provide what may be Sudan's only hope for peace.

Given the southern Sudanese complete rejection of the interpretation of Islam chosen by the government, and given the knowledge that the fundamentalism practiced by the northern Arab-Muslim Sudanese has no recourse for democratic values, we have to question the viability of Islam to serve as an ideology suitable for a modern nation-state to act in a humane manner towards its own citizens. After posing this question, we are presented with ample evidence that due to the element of *dhimmi* in this form of Islam, the current path of formal *sharia* and strict Islamic ideals cannot adequately address a diverse population in a manner deemed acceptable by the international community. Comparing incidents and ideology in Sudan with United Nations concepts of human rights and global ideals, we are left with no choice but to conclude that Sudan has implemented the concept of *dhimmi* in a way that leads to human rights abuse. Further, we are forced to the conclusion that Islam as it is understood by the Bashir regime and its supporters cannot function as the structural basis for a modern nation-state.

UNIVERSAL DECLARATION OF HUMAN RIGHTS

The United Nations Universal Declaration of Human Rights has a variety of general points it makes about the universality of human rights ideals. Whether or not those ideals are in fact universal is of some uncertainty. There is no doubt that the concept of human rights originated in the West, specifically in medieval Europe, and through various forms of colonialism and imperialism has been imposed on the international community.

Thus, while the basis of its applicability to non-western cultures can be questioned, for the purposes of this discussion we must accept the fact that the basic Western point of view is prevalent, and is inescapable in the contemporary debate. The United Nations Declaration is therefore taken as normative in the arena of politics, and decisions regarding the current status of any particular nation-state (including Islamic based states) is made taking into consideration the state's record in abiding by the Declaration's statements. Since Sudan is based entirely on 'Medinan Islam', the implicit role of *dhimmi* results in a series of conflicts with the accepted human-rights doctrine.

Obviously, the first problem encountered when comparing Sudanese *sharia* with the United Nations Declaration on Human Rights is that the Declaration specifies freedom of religion. Of course southern Sudanese are free to believe what they choose religiously, but the reality is that that choice can have repercussions in legal and social matters. Looking for specifics however, and taking our cue from the preamble to the UN Declaration, we observe that "... human beings shall enjoy freedom of speech ..."[75] Obviously, as the execution of Taha amply demonstrates, such freedom is not even remotely enjoyed in Sudan, even by someone effectively Muslim.

Although it would be relatively easy to proceed through the UN Declaration point by point and find an incident contrary to the Declaration's statements, we are more concerned with the under-girding, over-arching conflict between the ideal put forth by the Declaration, and the ideal put forth by "Medinan" Islam, which necessarily includes an implementation of *dhimmi*. Nevertheless, a few specific incidents pointing to the ideal of *dhimmi* in practice are useful to prove this point.

ZAKAT

According to the magazine Sudan Update, the average income for laborers is about S£500 (S£=Sudanese Pounds) per month. The Sudanese government has declared that the official poverty level is S£30,000. Due to one of the Pillars of Islam – *zakat*, the payment of taxes to support the poor – Muslims who fall below the poverty line can register in *zakat* centers, and instead of paying the *zakat*, can begin to receive financial relief funds. Laborers who have had to close their shops thus can continue to survive. Non-Muslim laborers are forced to pay taxes, and if they refuse to pay, their tools can be confiscated,[76] resulting in their inability to earn a living. However, these non-Muslims are not eligible for *zakat* relief. They are allowed to apply to the government for registration in United Nations relief programs such as Operation Lifeline Sudan, but have no recourse other than help external to the Muslim community. Thus, although there is no official doctrine of differing rights for Muslims and *dhimmis*, we see that the implicit doctrine is in line with historical implementation of the concept of *dhimmi*.

"WELFARE" OF MUSLIMS

At times, the only part of the concept of *dhimmi* that is recognizable is the priority given to Muslims, and the "protected people" aspect of *dhimmi* falls by the wayside. In August 1994, Sudan Update reported on the situation of 50,000 displaced people in Sudan as the Sudanese government halfheartedly tried to deal with its internal refugee and famine problems. Placing the welfare of its Muslim citizens above its Christian citizens, the government is attempting to reduce the drain on Khartoum's resources by expelling Christians from southern Sudan who sought refuge in Khartoum. The military raided homes in the middle of the night " ... to make sure the whole family is there. They're shoved onto trucks like cattle ... given nothing ... taken to refugee camps where nothing is prepared for them."[77]   This set of raids was not the first, nor anywhere near the largest. According to the United Nations, similar raids in 1992 expelled some 750,000 non-Muslims from Khartoum.[78]

In November 1994, the organization Human Rights Watch/Africa released a report entitled "In the Name of God", which details human rights abuses by the Sudanese government. Although the report does not specifically mention *dhimmi* as a concept currently applied by the government in Sudan, it does report on the specific Islamic source of these abuses. The report specifically states that "... the National Islamic Front's interpretation of *sharia*" results in restrictions on "... freedom of expression, association and belief ... in violation of internationally recognized standards of human rights." The report goes on to detail that these abuses are most obvious in the creation "...of a permanent underclass through its policies of marginalizing and segregating ... Southerners".[79] In essence, the report is a detailed analysis of the Sudanese regime's attempt to reinstate the practice of *dhimmi*.

SLAVERY

Perhaps the most startling information to come out of Sudan in recent months is the report that slavery is alive and thriving in the country. According to the London based Observer, Sudanese Muslim military officers are carrying on an illicit and highly profitable slave trade. The article recounts the experiences of a young southern girl who was abducted and sold into slavery. The article also tells he story of a young southern boy whose parents were killed by the Muslim army after which he was taken as a slave by a Muslim officer. Quoting Amnesty International officials, the article states that "Thousands [of southern, non-Muslim children] have probably been turned into slave chattels."[80] Although the Sudanese government continues to deny these allegations, the proof seems irrefutable. The reality of the slave trade points to the conscious demarcation by Sudanese Muslims of their fellow humans into categories, and these categories are in line with historical classifications involving Muslims, *dhimmis*, and slaves.

There are numerous examples of specific incidents which can be recounted and compared to concepts of *dhimmi*. Indeed, it seems as if there are such incidents with alarming frequency, but to list them all is not the point of this discussion. Such examples as cited above would seem to prove the point that although the Sudanese government is making no official claims to be implementing a policy on the basis of *dhimmi*, actions and policies being implemented under *sharia* are resulting in a society similar to that which Muslim fundamentalists envision existed in the caliphate period. It seems all too clear that these policies are at the root of the Sudanese problem, and that the role of *dhimmi* merely serves as one route to examining the crisis.

Conclusions

SUNNI ISLAM – AS IMPLEMENTED IN SUDAN – IS A PATH TO CIVIL WAR

We have seen that the promulgation of Islamic laws in Sudan under the aegis of implementing a formal interpretation of the *sharia* means creating a state in which there is no place for the southern Sudanese, because of the implicit role of *dhimmi* in those laws. As M. W. Daly points out in the essay "Islam, Secularism and Ethic Identity in the Sudan", such an interpretation of *sharia* ensures the continuation of civil war. The *sharia* as it is being implemented in Sudan "... excludes non-Muslims from the full rights of citizenship expected in a modern state ...".[81] Daly goes on to quote Abdullah Ahmed An-Na'im's statement given at a workshop on Sudanese identities: *sharia* (as interpreted in Sudan) "...does not conceive of the permanent residence of unbelievers within an Islamic state. At best, unbelievers may be allowed to stay under the terms of a special compact which extremely restricts their civil and political rights."[82]   Although neither An-Na'im nor Daly use the term, such a compact is obviously based on the concept of *dhimmi*.

IS THERE A SOLUTION?

We are left looking for a solution to the problem of integration in Sudan. As the *sharia* is not open to interpretation, as the death of Mahmoud Taha so clearly illustrates, it would seem that non-Muslims in Sudan are doomed to a life of second-class citizenship under an enforced *dhimmi* ideal. Yet such a system explicitly rejects statements in the United Nations Declaration on Human Rights, and such blatant disregard for these ideals will ultimately be addressed by the international community, perhaps in the form of embargoes and trade restrictions. It seems clear that another solution must be found.

Francis M. Deng writes in his book **War of Visions** that there are three possible solutions: the establishment of a new Sudanese identity that creates a common identity for Sudanese both in the Arab-Muslim north and the southern Sudan; creating a loose federal arrangement that provides for diversified coexistence; or partitioning Sudan into two distinct countries.[83] In looking at the partition proposal, one must bear in mind the Pakistan situation, and other situations world-wide where arbitrary division of land among religious and political boundaries has resulted in continued and often intensified conflict. In examining the idea of creating a loose federal or confederal arrangement, there still seems to be no room for compromise between southern Sudanese and northern "Meccan" fundamentalists. The possibility of creating a new common identity seems at best a far-fetched dream, as once again the specter of Muslim rejection of unbelievers raises its head.

The Republic of Sudan faces what seems an insurmountable problem: integrating religious fanaticism within a functioning nation-state. As recent world events illustrate, this is not a purely Sudanese, nor even a purely Muslim problem. Abortion rights activists in the United States clash with Christian fundamentalists resulting in deaths on both sides. In the United States however, there is clear distinction between church and state that at can at least provide a guideline for the legal debates which religious radicals and secularists are bringing to international attention. There is also the ideal of the individual and the individual's rights which plays a key role in these issues. No such church-state division exists in Islam, and thus debates involving religious issues are inherently political, social and moral as well as religious. Because of Islam's dedication to the ideal of the umma, such debates also become tied in with communal issues, rather than individual rights, and due to the role of concepts such as *dhimmi*, the very notion of rights is hard to bring up in an Islamic context.

AN ISLAMIC PROBLEM, NOT JUST SUDANESE

In the final analysis, the crisis facing Sudan is one facing all of Islam. The Muslims who are at the forefront of the Islamic resurgence are basing their interpretation of Islam on

'Medinan Islam', rather than 'Meccan'. In order for Islam to serve as the structural basis of a modern nation-state, Islam must come to terms with issues such as human rights and non-Muslims in the same geo-political arena, by looking back to the prophet's statements in Mecca prior to the *hijra*. This it seems can only be done through continued spiritual growth, as Muslims attempt to interpret their faith in light of increasing globalization.

Clearly, concepts such as *dhimmi* must fall by the wayside in that process, and Muslim thinkers such as Mahmoud Taha have pointed the way. Even in such a strict Islamic environment as Iran, progress is being made. Professor Abdol Karim Soroush, a well respected Muslim, has made statements regarding the present and future of Islam. "Islam and democracy are not only compatible, their association is inevitable."[84] Giving solid theological foundations for his arguments, Soroush points out that to be a true believer in any doctrine, including Islam, one must choose to believe. If any pressure exists to profess faith, as is the case when such concepts as *dhimmi* limit one's life and livelihood, then the prospect of false profession exists, and this is anathema. Therefore, the freedom to believe is a pillar of a modernizing Islam. That pillar, "this freedom," says Soroush, "is the basis of democracy."[85]

Drawing on the Islamic precedent of *ijtihad* – independent reasoning – Soroush is paving the path to an explicit division between church and state in Islam, the repercussions of which would be a completely new understanding of the function of Islam in the context of the nation-state and the emerging 'global village.' The combination of Soroush's ideas and Taha's arguments about what is true Islam, in the context of an increasing need for global cooperation, may provide Sudan and the rest of the Muslim "fundamentalist" world with their best hope for achieving Muhammed's goal: a world-wide spiritual community living in harmony with itself, and with its neighbors.

Notes

1. George Moyser, "Religion and Politics in the Modern World: An Overview", 1-27, Religion and Politics in the Modern World, George Moyser, ed. (London: Routledge, 1991), 4.

2. Abdelwahab El-Affendi, Who Needs an Islamic State? (London: Grey Seal, 1991), 66.

3. Karen Armstrong, A History of God (New York: Alfred A. Knopf, 1993), 133.

4. Karen Armstrong, A History of God (New York: Alfred A. Knopf, 1993), 134

5. John L. Esposito, Islam: The Straight Path (New York: Oxford University Press, 1991), 30-31.

6. John L. Esposito, Islam: The Straight Path (New York: Oxford University Press, 1991), 8.

7. Karen Armstrong, A History of God (New York: Alfred A. Knopf, 1993), 134.

8. John L. Esposito, Islam: The Straight Path (New York: Oxford University Press, 1991), 5.

9. John L. Esposito, Islam: The Straight Path (New York: Oxford University Press, 1991), 10.

10. Karen Armstrong, A History of God (New York: Alfred A. Knopf, 1993), 133.

11. Ibid.

12. Karen Armstrong, A History of God (New York: Alfred A. Knopf, 1993), 136.

13. John L. Esposito, Islam: The Straight Path (New York: Oxford University Press, 1991), 7.

14. John L. Esposito, Islam: The Straight Path (New York: Oxford University Press, 1991), 12.

15. John L. Esposito, Islam: The Straight Path (New York: Oxford University Press, 1991), 10.

16. Bernard Lewis, ed. The World of Islam: Faith, People, Culture (London: Thames and Hudson, 1976), 11.

17. John L. Esposito, Islam: The Straight Path (New York: Oxford University Press, 1991), 11.

18. Bernard Lewis, ed. The World of Islam: Faith, People, Culture (London: Thames and Hudson, 1976), 12.

19. John L. Esposito, Islam: The Straight Path (New York: Oxford University Press, 1991), 38.

20. John L. Esposito, Islam: The Straight Path (New York: Oxford University Press, 1991), 37-38.

21. John L. Esposito, Islam: The Straight Path (New York: Oxford University Press, 1991), 39.

22. Ibid.

23. Bernard Lewis, ed. The World of Islam: Faith, People, Culture (London: Thames and Hudson, 1976), 13

24. John L. Esposito, Islam: The Straight Path (New York: Oxford University Press, 1991), 38.

25. John L. Esposito, Islam: The Straight Path (New York: Oxford University Press, 1991), 45.

26. John L. Esposito, Islam: The Straight Path (New York: Oxford University Press, 1991), 42.

27. John L. Esposito, Islam: The Straight Path (New York: Oxford University Press, 1991), 41

28. *Quran*, as cited by James P. Piscatori, "Human rights in Islamic Political Culture", in The Moral Imperatives of Human Rights: A World Survey, ed. Kenneth W. Thompson. (Washington, DC: University Press of America, 1980), 139

29. Nazih Ayubi, Political Islam (London: Routledge, 1991), 253.

30. John L. Esposito, Islam: The Straight Path (New York: Oxford University Press, 1991), 52.

31. Nazih Ayubi, Political Islam (London: Routledge, 1991), 4-7.

32. Nazih Ayubi, Political Islam (London: Routledge, 1991), 4.

33. Bernard Lewis, ed. The World of Islam: Faith, People, Culture (London: Thames and Hudson. 1976), 34.

34. M. Hamidullah, The First Written Constitution in the World (Lahore: Sh. Muhammed Ashraf, 1981). 47.

35. CIA World Fact Book as presented on-line, accessible via the Internet.

36. Ibid.

37. Dunstan M. Wai, The African-Arab Conflict in the Sudan (New York: Africana Publishing Company, 1981), 16.

38. Dunstan M. Wai, The African-Arab Conflict in the Sudan (New York: Africana Publishing Company, 1981), 17.

39. Dunstan M. Wai, The African-Arab Conflict in the Sudan (New York: Africana Publishing Company, 1981), 26.

40. Ibid.

41. Mohamed Omer Beshir, The Southern Sudan: Background to Conflict (New York: Frederick A. Praeger, 1968), 9-10.

42. Ibid.

43. Dunstan M. Wai, The African-Arab Conflict in the Sudan (New York: Africana Publishing Company, 1981), 26.

44. Dunstan M. Wai, The African-Arab Conflict in the Sudan (New York: Africana Publishing Company, 1981), 29.

45. Oliver Albino, The Sudan: A Southern Viewpoint (London: Oxford University Press, 1970), 14-16.

46. Ibid.

47. Oliver Albino, The Sudan: A Southern Viewpoint (London: Oxford University Press, 1970), 16.

48. CIA World Fact Book as presented on-line, accessible via the Internet.

49. Dunstan M. Wai, The African-Arab Conflict in the Sudan (New York: Africana Publishing Company, 1981), 40-43.

50. CIA World Fact Book as presented on-line, accessible via the Internet.

51. Dunstan M. Wai, The African-Arab Conflict in the Sudan (New York: Africana Publishing Company, 1981), 45-47.

52. Dunstan M. Wai, The African-Arab Conflict in the Sudan (New York: Africana Publishing Company, 1981), 47.

53. Abdelwahab El-Affendi, Turabi's Revolution: Islam and Power in Sudan (London: Grey Seal, 1991), 36.

54. Abdelwahab El-Affendi, Turabi's Revolution: Islam and Power in Sudan (London: Grey Seal, 1991), 47.

55. Dunstan M. Wai, The African-Arab Conflict in the Sudan (New York: Africana Publishing Company, 1981), 56.

56. CIA World Fact Book as presented on-line, accessible via the Internet.

57. John O. Voll, "Sudan", 253-258 in Mews, Stuart, ed. Religion in Politics: A World Guide (London: Longman Group Ltd., 1989), 255.

58. CIA World Fact Book as presented on-line, accessible via the Internet.

59. John O. Voll, "Sudan", 253-258 in Mews, Stuart, ed. Religion in Politics: A World Guide (London: Longman Group Ltd., 1989), 255.

60. John O. Voll, "Sudan", 253-258 in Mews, Stuart, ed. Religion in Politics: A World Guide (London: Longman Group Ltd., 1989), 257-258.

61. Douglas H. Johnson, The Southern Sudan, Minority Rights Group Report No. 78 (London: MRG: 1988), 9.

62. Such documents include the press releases of the government on human-rights issues, the current "constitution" of the government.

63. This has been true since the 1983 September Laws were instituted by Numayri.

64. John O. Voll, "Fundamentalism in the Sunni Arab World: Egypt and Sudan", 345-402 in Fundamentalisms Observed, Volume I, Marty, Martin E. & R. Scott Appleby, eds. (Chicago: University of Chicago Press, 1991), 390.

65. Ibid.

66. John O. Voll, "Fundamentalism in the Sunni Arab World: Egypt and Sudan", 345-402 in Fundamentalisms Observed, Volume I, Marty, Martin E. & R. Scott Appleby, eds. (Chicago: University of Chicago Press, 1991), 367.

67. M. W. Daly, "Islam, Secularism, and Ethnic Identity in the Sudan", in Religion and Political Power, Gustavo Benavides and M. W. Daly, eds. (Albany: State University of New York Press, 1989), 86.

68. John O. Voll, "Fundamentalism in the Sunni Arab World: Egypt and Sudan", 345-402 in Fundamentalisms Observed, Volume I, Marty, Martin E. & R. Scott Appleby, eds. (Chicago: University of Chicago Press, 1991), 390.

69. M. W. Daly, "Islam, Secularism, and Ethnic Identity in the Sudan", in Religion and Political Power, Gustavo Benavides and M. W. Daly, eds. (Albany: State University of New York Press, 1989), 88.

70. Marty, Martin E. & R. Scott Appleby, "Introduction - The Fundamentalism Project: A User's Guide", vii-xiii in Fundamentalisms Observed, Volume I, Marty, Martin E. & R. Scott Appleby, eds. (Chicago: University of Chicago Press, 1991), vii-ix.

71. Francis M. Deng, War of Visions: Conflict of Identities in the Sudan (Washington, D.C.: The Brookings Institution, 1995), 125.

72. Francis M. Deng, War of Visions: Conflict of Identities in the Sudan (Washington, D.C.: The Brookings Institution, 1995), 125-126.

73. For instance, the texts of Medina encourage forcible conversion to Islam and speak of jihad, whereas the texts of Mecca are oriented towards peaceful cooperation and voluntary conversion. See Francis M. Deng, War of Visions: Conflict of Identities in the Sudan (Washington, D.C.: The Brookings Institution, 1995), 125-128.

74. Francis M. Deng, War of Visions: Conflict of Identities in the Sudan (Washington, D.C.: The Brookings Institution, 1995), 125-126.

75. The United Nations Universal Declaration of Human Rights, preamble.

76. Peter Verney, ed. Sudan Update Vol. 5 No. 10 (2 June 1994), 3.

77. Peter Verney, ed. Sudan Update Vol. 5 No. 13 (3 August 1994), 2.

78. Peter Verney, ed. Sudan Update Vol. 5 No. 13 (3 August 1994), 3.

79. Peter Verney, ed. Sudan Update Vol. 5 No. 20 (30 November 1994), 4.

80. Peter Verney, ed. Sudan Update Vol. 6 No. 7 (15 May 1995), 2-3.

81. M. W. Daly, "Islam, Secularism, and Ethnic Identity in the Sudan", in Religion and Political Power, Gustavo Benavides and M. W. Daly, eds. (Albany: State University of New York Press, 1989), 95.

82. Ibid.

83. Francis M. Deng, War of Visions: Conflict of Identities in the Sudan (Washington, D.C.: The Brookings Institution, 1995), 484-517.

84. Robin Wright, "Islam confronts its Luther in Iran", The Guardian (1 February 1995).

85. Ibid.

www.ingramcontent.com/pod-product-compliance
Lightning Source LLC
Chambersburg PA
CBHW020518030426
42337CB00011B/456